With Love, from Studewood

Y. Zambrano

Copyright © 2025 **Y. Zambrano, M.S.**
Cover Art and Illustrations © 2025
Sandra X. Solis-Cardenas, M.A., CCC-SLP
Editor: **Ashley Jane/Ashley Jane Aesthetics**

All rights reserved. No part of this publication may be reproduced, distributed, or transmitted in any form or by any means, electronic, mechanical, photocopying, recording, or otherwise without prior written permission unless for the purposes of reviewing.

With Love, from Studewood/Y. Zambrano
1st Edition 2025
ISBN: 9798218820312

Before you turn the page,
sit in stillness.
Close your eyes and quiet your mind.
Embrace the uniqueness that spills into you.
You are loved.
You are the light.
Let the sound of your soul lead the way.
As you rise once again,
you become new with the morning sun.
Beautiful is you.

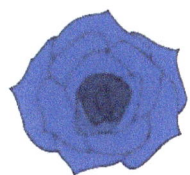

♡ and the love letters were from *Studewood ST 1300 1400* me with love filling heart with love love profess you make heart sing forever and always yours truly poet Lynette

And the letters were written

from Studewood

Dreams

Couldn't sleep.
I must be awake in your dreams.
So, I asked the angels to surround you
while you sleep.

A.M.

It's 5:10 a.m.,
and you hit snooze again
just to roll over
and kiss me
and stay in bed
for another 10 of these morning minutes.

Paint The Sky

Hymns.
A symphony painted in the sky.
Songs of Solomon.
A valley of lilies.
Do you feel this presence?
It is a spiritual awakening.
Breathe in all those colors.
Let it fall.
Carry them on your sleeve,
and speak to me so vibrantly.

Love in December

The wind of shadow whispers
are on a dreamtime eve of cranberry drops.
It's pouring warmth of winter onto our arms.
Me on you,
me with you,
flowing with cinnamon wishes.
I love it here,
because we are here.

Colors

These black and white walls
turn to color when you enter.

Gravity

As our lips touched,
I knew he was my gravity.

This heart,

She always knew and loved you all along.

**Midnight
flames
ignite
from
a touch.**

As I looked into the flame,
I said a prayer that
whispered your name.

Same as One

Don't think I don't see.
We are one and the same,
    you in me and I in you.
It has never felt so right,
inhaled breaths in the same intake,
streaming through each other's veins.

A knot that ties
is what you and I are joined by.

Endless Cascades

Wished away from falling cascades.
Love is,
at this time,
rushing me.
Power of hearts.
As sole.

I do love you.

Garnet and Gold

He's of garnet
    and pure gold.

My Beloved,
across the Atlantic,
   here I'll be.

Spring

Warm candy rain,
as the balloons blew in a spring lullaby.

Twin Flames

I kissed your lips
and suddenly I knew.
I knew my soul had been searching for you.
All along,
I think I knew.
I knew that I always belonged to you.

I kissed your lips and suddenly you knew.
You knew that I was always meant for you.

Two souls into one.
Our future has begun.

Hearts Smile

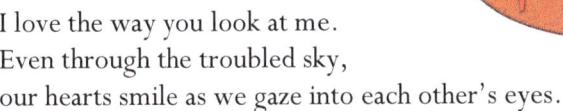

I love the way you look at me.
Even through the troubled sky,
our hearts smile as we gaze into each other's eyes.

Cinnamon

You feel like rain,
like the fire from an autumn night kiss.
A touch of apple cinnamon.
A memory like a perfect old rose.
This flower I once didn't know.

He is the moon,

and

I am his star.

Dashing

For now,
we can shut the whole world out.
We can be together.
You are the world,
      just dashing.

Reincarnation

When you've found the one,
suddenly it all makes sense.
The familiar feeling that you keep hearing about.
You and I have been here before.
I have known you all my life.
Your eyes,
oh, those eyes,
are the same as mine.
I see the reflections from each of our past lives,
every single time that I have loved you,
and here we are again.
We find each other every single time.
You make my whole soul glow.
This is our truth.
We give each other life.

Love You

Oh,
how my soul loves yours,
even at a distance,
but for now I send you love notes
until we are joined sooner than we know.

One by one,

each scar fell from the touch of your sun-kissed lips.

I am more than the scars laid.

When I

>look to the deepest of places,
>I find you in them.

When I go within,
I find your gentle nature curving
like rose water.

>And when I close my eyes,
>I feel your love on my tongue.

Soul of Notes

Nothing ever wounded when it came to
these words that we speak into each other's soul.
As we come to the dance of streaming music notes,
suddenly
we fall in love with one another's sides.

I am that I am, I am self love
beautiful
I love you forever
mucho tiempo
changing and evolving
light vessel
blessed be everyday forever

Light of the world
within myself
once upon a time
Light our volumes Eternally
belongs to me
Energy
changing and evolving
I am
implement
fearless
Creative
love
I am that

*You are written
in rose gold
right inside my soul.*

Home

This place I lay my head:
his home,
my home.
A place where we both feel whole.
Our home,
in this home.
The place to fall the deepest.
Within this home
is where our hearts lie.

Messages

Upon my flesh,
he stamped his name across my chest.
Love letters all over me.
Music notes whispered straight into me.
The sweetest poetry I've ever known.
Imprints spoke of his desires.
He printed his name all around my neck,
a canvas painted with every mark.
Oh,
how gently he kisses.
I placed my lips onto his.
Messages he fed.
Write whatever you may wish.
Love letters and music notes
I now scattered onto him.

Given Name

And
before you,
here I stand with a promise
as I hold your hand.
A promise from a name.
Just your name.

There are flickers and flames

between our souls.

I Come Back

In the distance,
the haunting winds
are a midnight garden.
I come back passing through
to the place of the flower
I dropped for you.

Boudoir

Your sparkling red-light
floods entryways.
But the tempting windows we see
foretell of who stayed.
A crystal chandelier
overlooking gilded mementos promising bliss.
Familiar,
yet fresh air mercifully soaking it all up.
Hours and days curl up with secrets
in a whirl of linden trees.

Perfect

Love and all those flaws,
and yet,
you're still perfect to me.

Crescent Days

Even in the day,
the crescent moon comes through
just to find you.

The moonlight

shines upon your lips

as we kiss.

Sleep and Dreams

In between sleep and dreams,
I can hear the music of you and me.

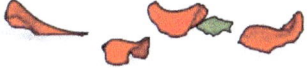

Autumn Rain

Lined with the leaves under an autumn evening,
the showers of its maple rain hit the parts of me
I give to you.

Rain

I won't let the rain come pouring down on you.

Stories of You

Your stories still hang.
They stay.
They've been staying.
The stories,
they go on and on.
They stay.
They live every night
inextricably linked *to you.*

The King and I

Under the moonlight,
I dance as the lion watches over.
Lovers from many lifetimes ago
meeting here once again.
Fire and air,
here we are.
The king and I.
And so,
it is.

Amor,

To thee I only look to.
All the ways of reasons why:
my light,
my sky,
my sweet ocean.
The embers burn as one.
In harmony, we two only exist.
To the end, I will go,
and into the night, I will be.
All the ways of love are here.

My Love,

I love thee,
forevermore.

Home of Love

And together,
we will raise only love.

Black Shirt

His black shirt,
I wear when the sun has set.
His shirt,
I press against my face.

Black shirt,
inhale through my skin.

Black shirt,
whisper those same words to me.

Black shirt,
gently be.
His shirt,
I embrace.

Black shirt.
Just his black shirt.

Unspoken

Hold me while we are here,
so, the things unsaid can be said.

Sunrose Lovers

There are fragments washed in a sun shadow.
The line read in dance storms from
its caged rose.
Formed heartbeats and secrets falling close.
I am the sun rose you seek,
liquid petals on each part of our fleshy tissue,
choosing those for our soul.

This Moment

My breaths are heavy.
I wonder if he can hear the thunder of my heartbeat.
So many thoughts,
it's a maze of wonder.
Sitting closely by his side,
his hand is right next to mine.
Should I rest my head on his shoulder?
I'll just let him take the lead.
I have so much I want to say,
but the words simply won't obey.
His energy is strong.
Nothing at all feels off.
Has fate finally led us this way?
He makes me feel more than safe.
I think I will start praying for him from this day.
Everyday.

You're a breath of music

and

the only tune I want to listen to.

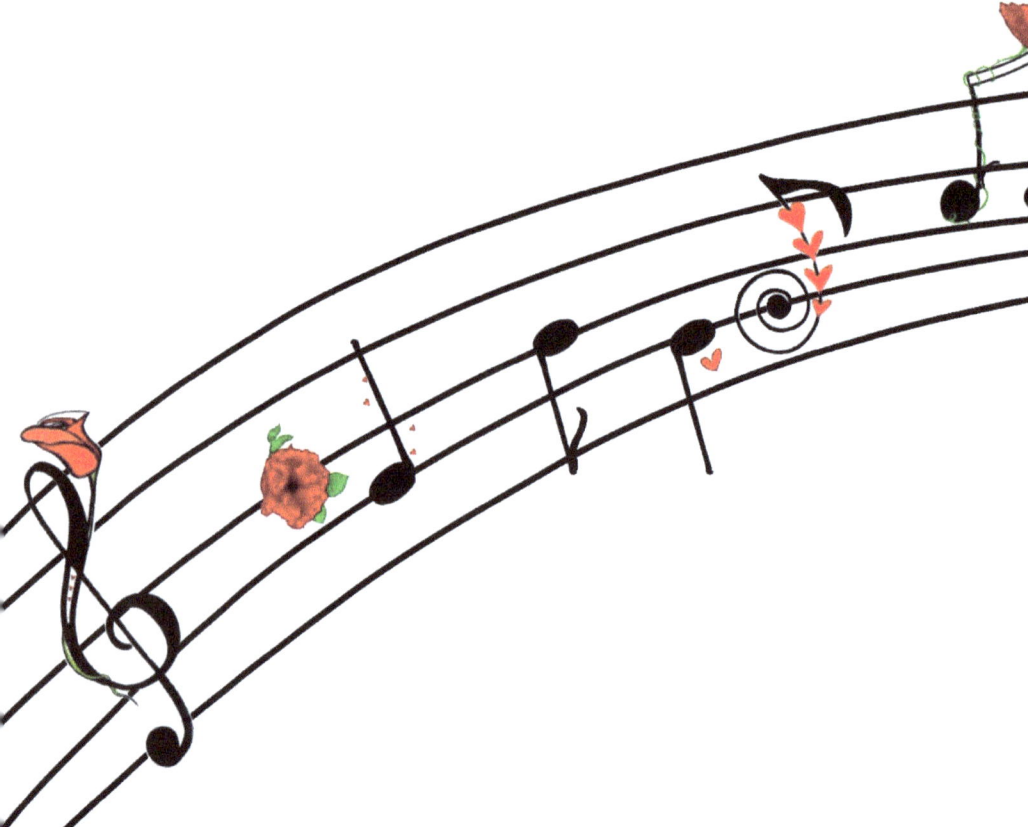

Dance with me in the middle

of these midnight streets.

Southern Ride

He was special,
so, I wrote him a letter
wondering if he'd come.
In later months,
he came for me.
I left and took a southern ride with him.
Sweetwater highways made with moonshine.
Out here is where we got married,
and I will love him until the end of time.

Ocean Deep

These scars are ocean deep.
Therefore,
so is this love.

Scars of Love

The one who has the scars
 I only see beauty in him.

The Softest Sound

My heart speaks softly of every letter of his name.

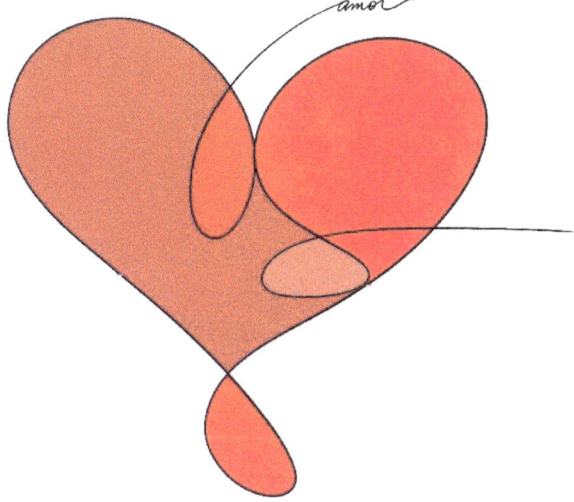

Here

And again,
before I knew.
Here,
we became one.
A final time.
And I knew I would say
I do.
Your embrace.
is the only thing I want to drown in.

Here we are.

Lustered

Fields of emeralds flow through me.
Time stamped the lettered lines it blew in.
Breathless in between the cycles.
And in the end,
it was him and I.
And those whispered breaths began to luster.

One Heart

And I found that our hearts beat as one.

Awoken

He feeds my soul.
Yet,
it's more than sexual.
He has awakened the places I have never known.

Ivy Chanel

I sleep underneath your breath.
Draped in a collection of Chanel.
18k gold rush from a drop of elegance.
Two faces melting into
infused fragrance.
Thoughts carried in ivy.

Him

For Him,
she will travel the depths of the blue sea.
Climb the heights of the mountains.
Journey across that elongated mile.
Walk the ground that now bleeds
from the cuts of her feet.
Face the changing of seasons.
And with eyes wide open,
she will stare time down
until it falls at their side.
But just for Him.

*My love for you is as deep
as the great ocean of pure blue.*

*Your smell,
your touch,
the warmth of you,
is planted in me.*

*Forever,
you are my heart.
Forever,
I love you.*

*I will kiss you goodnight
while the moon lights up our nights.*

*For our love creates miracles,
for our love is destined,
for our love has brought us together through time.*

I Asked,

"What am I supposed to do?"

Love him, HE told me.
His soul carries yours.
Pray for him.
Be his.
You shall give him peace.
Love him unconditionally.
You are the light to this man's life.

And then,
lead him to me,
for he will understand his destiny.

It's You

I'm just looking for someone as wild as me,
someone whose shadow matches mine,
knowing that each of our demons
will be able to recognize.

Is it you?
I think it's you.

Yes!
I know it's you.

Peace and Sleep

I laid my head on your chest.
I heard your heartbeat
and I knew the rest.
I kissed you as we slept.
I gripped your arm tightly.
Peace then allowed me to rest.

Day and Night

At night when the town is hushed
and sleep carries trances away,
there are those that are wakeful,
counting stars
while wishing on a few that stayed.
And as the sun begins to rise,
the hopefulness carried
from last night becomes anew.
With childlike eyes and playful hands,
this is how each day should begin.

Liquid Zen

Pearl white sheets he lays me on.
Fire and furry are between our eyes.
Map my body.
Stain my lips.
Purify me.
One need.
He's careful with me,
dripping drops,
each one here only I can hear.
Saltwater baths are like violin strings onto our bodies.
Taking it all in while he takes me.

Origami Hearts

Fold by fold,
creased in such a way
that every heartbeat matches what we see.
Origami of adoration.
A Valentine to my dearest inamorato.
Words spilled from the ink.
Darling,
in our hearts is where it loomed.

I Will Love You

I will love you in the rain.
I will love you through the pain.
I will love you at noon.
I will love you to the moon.
I will love you at dawn.
I will love you while we sing your favorite song.
I will love you through the calm.
I will love you if you can't go on.
I will love you during the night.
I will love you with all my might.
And I will love you,
just you
                                   all along…

A Love Language

Profoundly,
touch me.
Let me feel you with me.
Rather,
here, which I choose,
show me all the ways of love.
I hunger for the language of you.

Skin Of Love

If you look closely,
his love story is painted all over me.

King and Queen

He sits on this throne
while she sits by his side as the reigning Queen.
Two souls that made it to destiny.
Enlightened,
they both came to be
joined by a red thread.
Forever is what they will make this,
sighted through eyes of Love.
For they will peacefully be,
Eternally.

Underneath the full moon,
I saw a glimpse of me and you.

Pearlescent Tears

As the rain arrived,
it washed away the yesterday.
Indigo sights
furnished hope to a few
as we stand here
with
pearlescent tears.

Sunset Lovers

Whiskey on my breath,
a sunset with my lover,
his air coming down my spine.
Touch me.
Take control here.
Sun drops of love,
sun kisses falling like sand.
Here,
we speak in happiness.
Sunflowers around us dance to the sounds of us.
A love here,
surrounding in summer love.

Before

Before I felt those lips,
before that first kiss,
before I felt your touch,
and before I came to know such,
your name,
your image,
the familiarity of you
was already planted in me.

Healed

All our lonely nights
and the darkness we carry inside
has brought us together to breathe new life.

It was

    the way he looked at me
    and how tightly he held me.

                    It was how he waited on me
              and how he held the umbrella for me.

It was those kisses on my forehead
and how he laid his head on me.

                  It was how soundly he fell asleep next to me
                      and how peacefully I came to be.

A Song

The beat of my heart
is the very song that beats with yours.

In every one of our existences,

we shall dance together

endlessly.

Patience

Years to find this.
Years to feel this.
Years to have this.
Years to know this.
Years to reach this.
Years to be this.
Years.
I've waited for this.

Summer

Suddenly summer becomes us.
Bourbon roses come rushing down
my spine from the heatwave.
I sit alone with my thoughts to a sun shadow
and write out its poetry.
The longing from the days enters the nights
to be held.
I write about these times and let the
tenderness fill me whole.

As the weather shifts,

it fills in the language of you.

January Moon

In the middle of the fog,
unfold
the she-wolf
as the moon gets a little closer on a cold January.

Run Wild

Don't tame her.
Just run wild with her.

She is where beauty breathes.

And

out of

the dark

arose

her art.

I broke **free**
from what I used to be covered in.

*Warm and wild
just like the laughter of a child.*

Woman (part I)

As women,
I think we have all been there before,
having loved,
loved so much that was all wrong,
but always trying to fix those things,
even when it wasn't your fault.

Thinking,
maybe it will get better?
Maybe things will change?

Act this way,
but not that way.

Say this,
but don't say that.

Just see what happens,
but it's never anything good.
Even after all the same signs.

And then we go into this.
Forgetting about our own happiness.
That happens sometimes.
Especially when you both fall in love so young.

But really,
it was never love to begin with.

And in a way,
what we women who have been there before
must understand
is that **wrong** love is the greatest teacher
life can give us.

A teacher to strengthen us,
to see our self-worth,
to place us on our path,
and to help us grow in ways
we never would have imagined before.

Woman (part II)

And after,
I became soft.
My soul turned to gold.
I woke up beautiful and with wings,
as the butterfly in me finally emerged.

So, woman,
I bet you speak differently now,
and you even walk differently.
Your eyes see things that you once could not.
Woman, I am you.
I have been you,
and we are the same.
I recognize that glow
and the way that you move.
So, I smile when I see you.

The pieces are the same,
so, be proud of that heartache and pain.
It does fall away.
Let the freedom bring you to your true self.
Darling songs begin.

And now,
I am soft.
The words that I speak are so soft.
How I touch is soft
and I am soft,
because I have been where it was most rough.

Wildflower Mothers

Created from the roots
of the mothers who came from before,
traveling through time
in each step.

Hips shift in grace.
Voice speaks with courage.
A womb so soft as it gives life.
Eyes tell many stories.

Mother of mothers
carrying each other
through every vein
like wildflowers.

Echoes

There is a hum coming from
the internal parts of me,
all in waves of light and midnight dust.
I closely listen to the guidance from spirit.
Gold flakes turn to me with echoes that
sing me to sleep.
A new day dawns,
filtered in sunrise.

Aquarius Woman

Queen of her realm,
she bathes under the moon in a sea of stars.
Her alluring beauty will capture your heart.
Let her run wild with you,
rebel soul,
deep soul.
She's a spiritual being.
Love is the only language she softly speaks.
She will awaken you.
And with a forest in her,
discover the enchantment
of the Aquarius Woman.

I am (Woman)

I am a song.
I am the light in the night.
I am a rose.
I am water that purifies.
I am those soft rain drops.
I am thunder.
I am this.
I am that.
I am beauty.
I am where love lies.
I am a butterfly.
I am those thunderous midnight seas.
I am the air.
I am a woman.

I am soft in sunrise.

Beautiful You

Skin

I am in love
with the brown
that I am in.

*The rough patches
of my path
have softened
the internal parts
of my being.*

Spirit Daughter

I am a daughter of the waters.
Under her sun,
she kisses my brown skin.
Gentle waves align my hips
and rise to call my ancestors in.
Water me gently.
Truths are spoken,
invoking everything taught to me.
Within these beautiful hours,
I wash from head to feet,
silent words whispering through me.
I am home.
It tastes like love here.

Seashells

The sunlight runs through my hair
as I collect seashells.
A rush of waves at my feet
calls to me.
Every sound nourishes my soul.
My skin radiates when I am here,
becoming one of everything when
the sun and sea meet.

Stardust Rose

Strawberry roses
are in the curve of her hips,
a haven written with warmth.
She recites her psalm with the
softest inhale.
Her eyes tell a story filled with
dandelions and daffodils.
With every move,
she leaves behind
her stardust trail for you to find.

How does it end?

   Well,
   with you and I.

      Just the two of us
      running as one.

You are the poetry
I only choose to read.

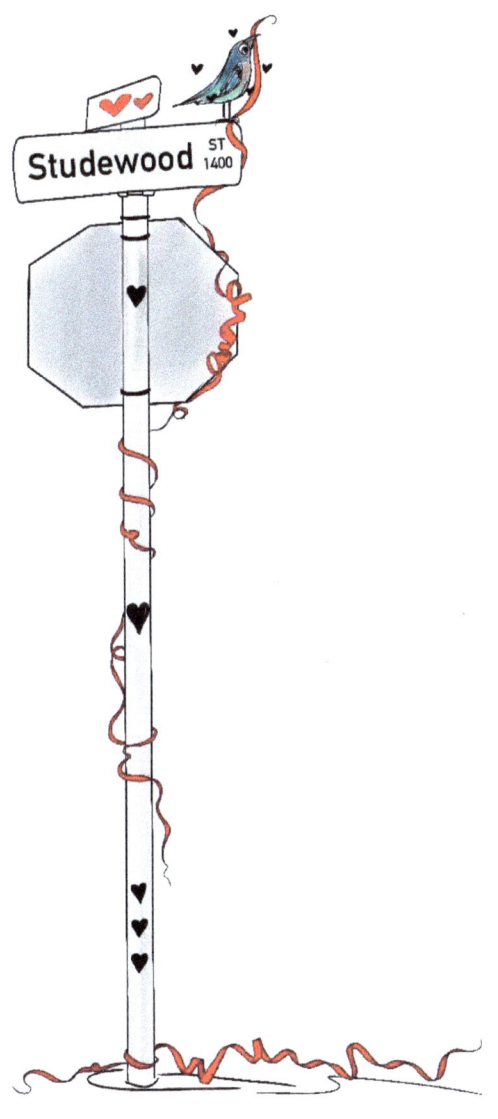

Acknowledgements

I want to thank those that were involved in creating my second poetry book.

Thank you to my wonderful editor, Ashley Jane for her patience and insight through the process of building this book. Collaborating with her is always a pleasure. To my amazing, dear friend, and illustrator, Sandra Solis-Cardenas for creating the magic behind the beautiful illustrations. I wouldn't have it any other way!

And of course, thank you to my readers who picked up this poetry book to read and view the gorgeous illustrations that accompanies each piece. Your support means the world to me.

I am honored that you chose this poetry book to have in your home.

About the Author

Y. Zambrano is a writer born and raised in Houston, Texas. She received her B.S. in Psychology from the University of Houston, Downtown and later completed her master's degree from Lamar University. She began writing poetry in 2013 as a therapeutic approach which has led her to creating her own art in poetry form.

She has previously published one poetry book titled Blue Roses and a children's book called Sleep with Night in collaboration with her friend and illustrator, Sandra Solis-Cardenas.

www.ingramcontent.com/pod-product-compliance
Lightning Source LLC
Chambersburg PA
CBHW050735010526
44107CB00010B/859